I0410660

THE INNER CIRCLE TRADER ICT FOREX TRADING CONCEPT

The Full ICT Day Trading Model, the Order Block Trading, the Market Structure , the Price Action Trading Concept, and the Top Down Analysis of the Smart Money Concept

MASON ANDERSON

Copyright © 2023 STEVE GREY. All rights reserved

ICT PRICE ACTION CONCEPTS

Only a small handful of price action situations are really crucial to us. These fundamental components serve as the structure for our trading setups. All of our setups are predicated on the price action's four main components: consolidation, expansion, reversal, and retracement.

Price always advances from consolidation to expansion rather than from consolidation to retracement or reversal. After an expansion, there can be a retracement or a turnabout, then another expansion or consolidation. That explains why it keeps happening again and time again.

Orderblocks, fair value gaps and liquidity voids, liquidity pools and stop runs, and equilibrium serve as the framework's reference points.

Expansion and Orderblocks

Price usually moves swiftly or expands from equilibrium points, leaving an orderblock in its wake. We seek for a reversal entry when the price contacts or breaks through the orderblock later, when it bounces back or goes in the direction of the orderblock.

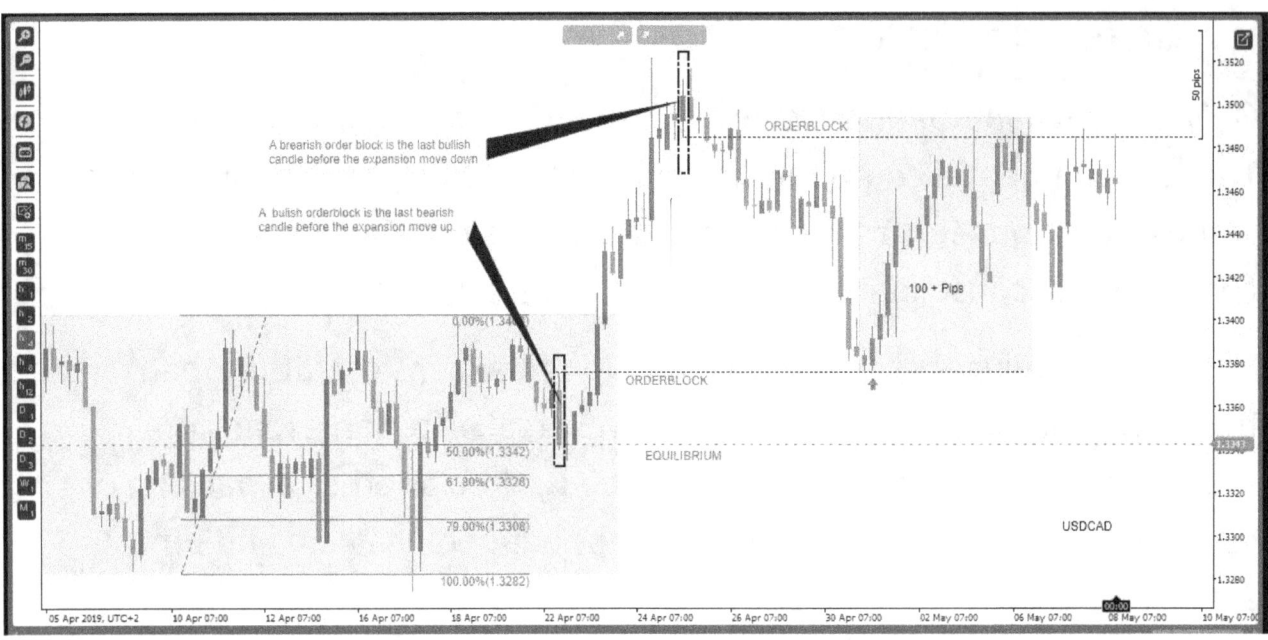

USDCAD H4 Chart

Retracement and Fair Value Gaps and Liquidity Voids

The least traded portions of the range are the enormous candles that appear after a sharp run in Price. Price Action left behind by sudden price runs is permeable and often fills in later. It is sometimes possible to notice these minute gaps by opening a 1 minute or 5 minute chart. A liquidity hole or lack of market liquidity is what is being experienced here.

Fair valuation happens when price trades back within of its current range and returns to levels it has previously left, sometimes due to an orderblock. The smart money regularly buys new short bets while selling existing long holdings in this market. Because of this, it's a great location to make money or take on a new position.

A fair value gap exists when a price deviates from a specific level and only a very small amount of the price movement is regarded to have one direction. These might provide very potent possibilities for profit-taking or brand-new setups.

USDCHF H4 Chart

Reversals and Liquidity Pools and Stop Runs

When price trades in the opposite direction from where it had been after being rejected, this is known as a reversal, and it often causes a change in the trend's direction. This indicates that Smart Money has reached a specific number of stops and that there will now be a significant change in the new direction. When there are liquidity pools that may be discovered as buy stops or sell stops at peak formations, clear highs, and clear lows, this is what we anticipate occurring.

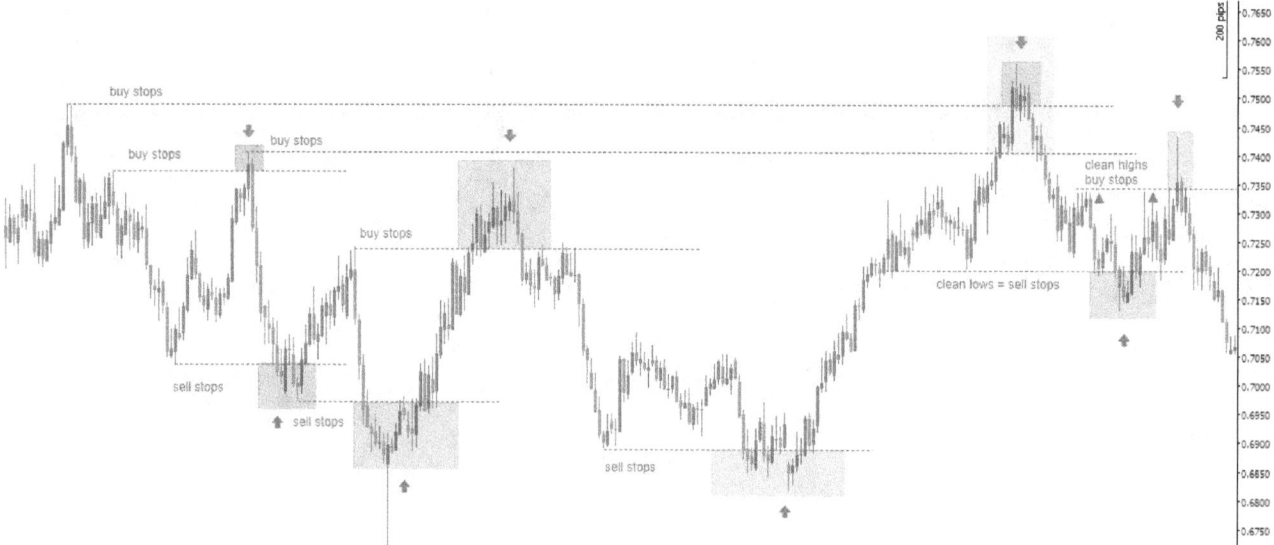

MACRO REVERSALS: NZDUSD D1 Chart

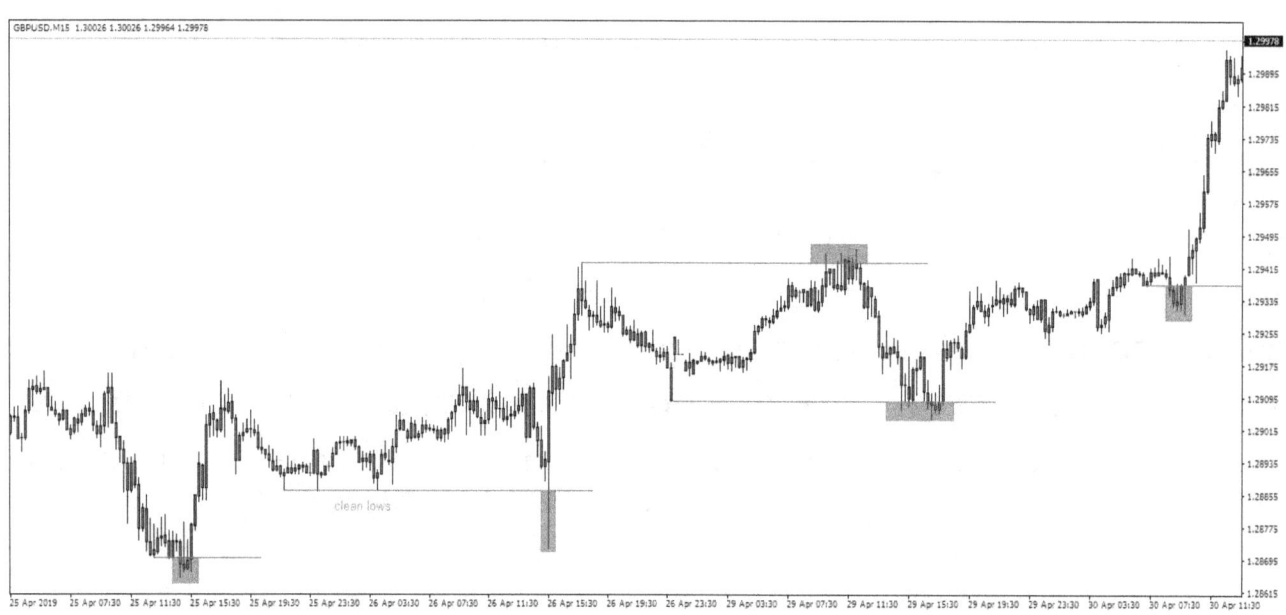

MICRO REVERSALS: GBPUSD 15M Chart

Equilibrium, Premium and Discount

After a market has declined and has begun to reprice upward, we look
for a gain of more than 50% or equilibrium for the market to be at a
premium, which creates strong short setups. After a market has surged

higher and begins to retrace lower, we look for a loss below equilibrium or 50% for the market to be at a discount, which frames strong long setups. For this, we make use of the Fibonacci tool.

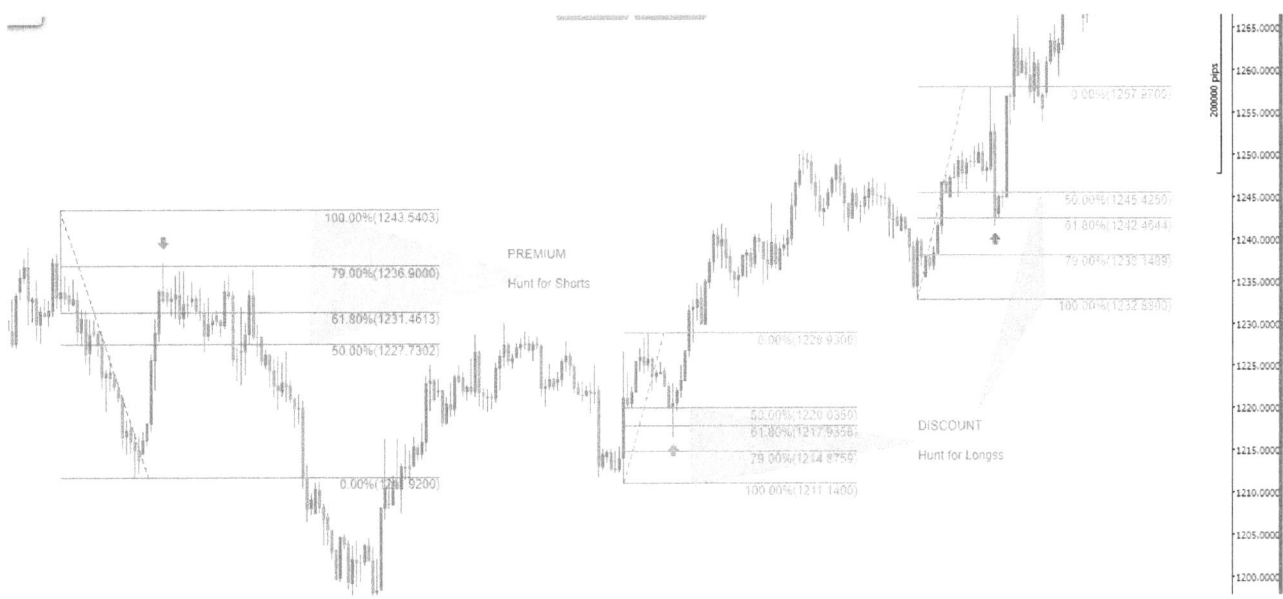

XAUUSD H4 Chart

Low Resistance Liquidity Run

When Price can move a liquid area with just little resistance. This is often located just below or slightly above an Old High. Prices will often rise sharply after the announcement of an economic news release. The foundation of high probability setups is the belief that the market will encounter minimal resistance prior to reaching distinct liquidity pools.

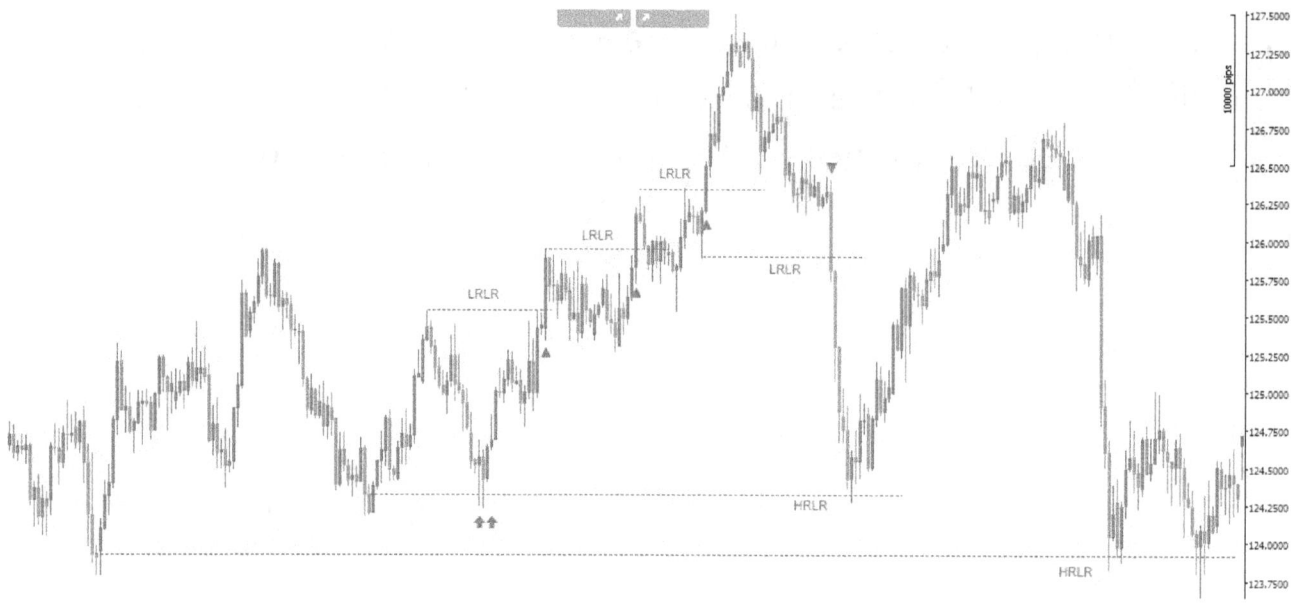

EURJYP H4 Chart

Defining Order Blocks

Breaker Block: Bearish

Best seen during extended to moderate downtrends. A bearish breaking block is a bearish range or a Down Close Candle in the most recent Swing Low before an Old High is broken. When the same swing low is broken after purchasers who bought at this low do so, they will try to minimize their loss. When the price returns to the swing low, this is a bearish trade scenario to consider.

Vice Versa for Bullish Breakers.

Rejection Blocks. Bearish
A bearish rejection block occurs when a price high has formed with long wicks on the candlestick highs and price climbs peak above the candle(s)' body to deplete buy side liquidity before price descends lower.

Vice Versa for Bullish RB

Another kind of rejection block is the purchase or sale of turtle soup. This happens as a result of a bearish run on buy-side liquidity or a bullish rush on sell-side liquidity.

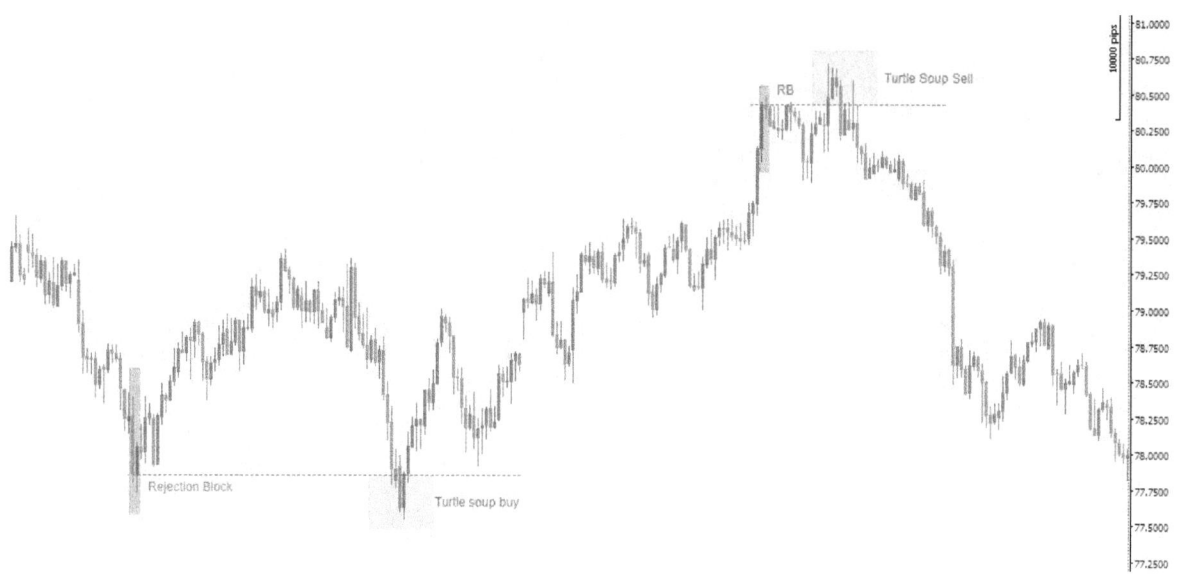

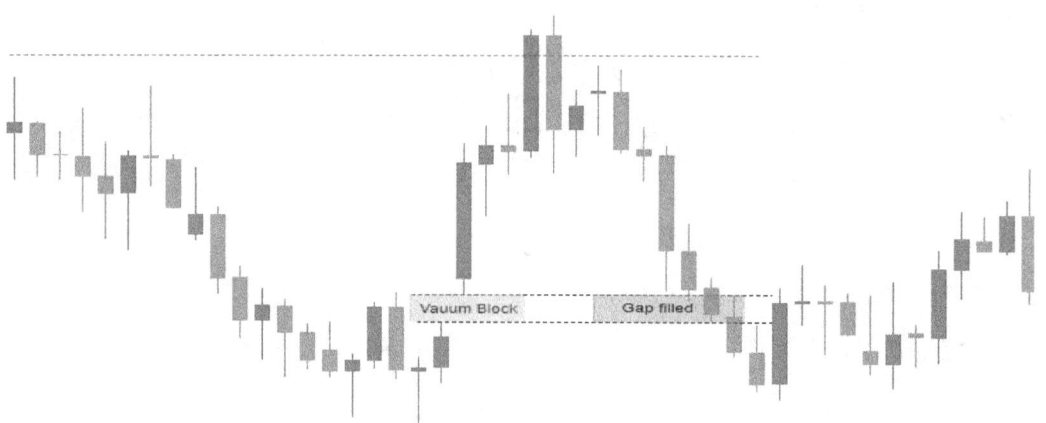

Vacuum Block: Bullish Gap

This is the outcome of a price action volatility event. The gap develops as a consequence of a "vacuum" of liquidity that follows an event. A session beginning in futures or NFP [Nonfarm Payroll] might produce a vacuum block.

Vice Versa for Bearish Gap **Institutional Swing Points**

There are primarily 2 types: failure swings and halt runs. These are the most lively and potent.

Stop Runs: When the market reaches or falls just below a pivotal level without immediately reacting, it indicates that there will be another run deeper before the turn. The opportunity is best taken when the short-term Market Structure breaking point is retested after the reversal. The initial run on stops is excellent in an intermediate-term price action; the smart money will want to remove the aggressive following stops.

Failure Swings: The market retraces after first passing through a ley level and rejecting the new price level before attempting to mount another push to retest the new price level. When a market structure breaking point or the first important level is once again tested after a reversal. That is the best moment to take advantage of the chance.

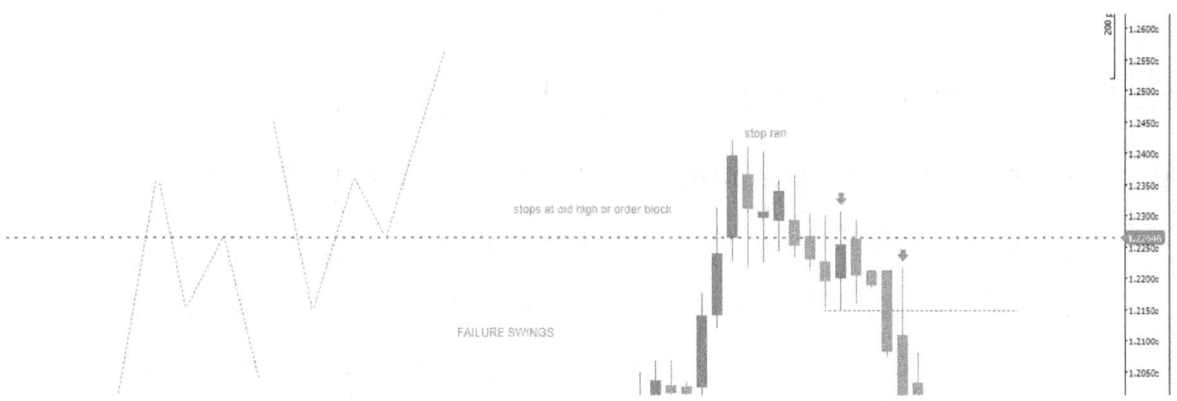

Framing Low Risk and High Reward Setups

Big Picture

    1. Macro market analysis of markets with inflation and deflation.

    2. Analysis of Interest Rates

    Rate increases, rate decreases, and unanticipated change.

    3. Intermarket Evaluation

    Commodity price index CRB and major currency index USDX.

    4. Seasonal factors

    Seasonal bullish and bearish trends.

Intermediate Picture

1) Monthly, weekly, and daily chart analysis using top-down analysis.

2) Bullish and Bearish COT Data Hedging by Intelligent Money and Historical Extreme Levels.

3) Extreme Bullishness and Bearishness in the Market.

Short Term

    a. Analysis of Correlation

SMT evaluations of the USDX and associated pairs.

b. Time and Price Theory Weekly and Daily Ranges, Quarterly and Monthly Effects, and Time of Day.

c. Institutional Order Flow, Liquidity Seeking, and Market Efficiency Paradigm - Inter-Bank Price Delivery Algorithm (IPDA).

Choice of the Time Frame and Model Setups

Monthly Charts - Trading Position

Swing Trading Weekly Charts

Daily Charts - 4 Hour or Less Short-Term Trading - Day Trading

Trading simply in the direction of the Monthly & Weekly Chart direction is the setup model for a trend trader.

Swing Trader: Trading the medium-term price movement on the daily chart.

Trading reversal patterns at market extremes is known as contrarian trading.

Short-term traders trade the weekly ranges for a period of one to five days.

Swing trading intraday with exits by 2:00 pm New York time, for day traders.

Identifying Institutional Sponsorship

Look for the following for lengthy setups:
1. Price Displacement in the Higher Time Frame: Reversals, Expansion, or Return to Fair Value.
2. Price Inequality Over The Intermediate Term - Move To Discount or Sell Side Liquidity Run.
3. Above-market short-term buy liquidity is ideal for partnering with long exits to sell to.
4. The impact of the time of day, such as the London Open Low or the New York Low Formation

Contrary for Shorts.

Institutional Market Structure

What Is Institutional Market Structure, in General?

1) The examination of assets that are associated or that are negatively connected.

2) To ascertain what the "Smart Money" is acquiring or dispersing.

3. It is simple to analyze currencies using Institutional Market Structure and the USDX.

4) It is important to examine each price change to see whether Market Symmetry supports it. B. How Can We Recognize Institutional Forex Market Structure?

1) Evaluate each change in the USDX's price against the foreign currency you trade. 2) Expect a smaller price fluctuation in foreign currency pairings as the USDX trades higher. 3) Smart Money is trading if USDX or a foreign currency fails to move symmetrically..

USDX SMT Divergence

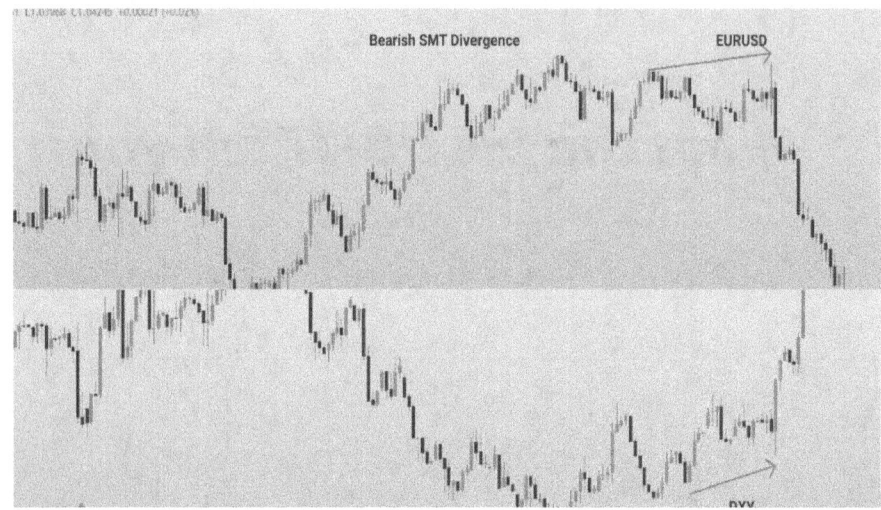

Under symmetrical market conditions, the XXXUSD pairings result in a greater high/LL when the USDX reaches a lower low/HH. The underlying trend is now "likely" to continue, according to this confirmation. It is thus improbable and foolish to attempt to trace reversal tendencies in this circumstance.

Under non-symmetrical market circumstances, when the USDX makes a lower low/HH and the XXXUSD pairs fail to make a higher high/LL, the present price action is not confirmed, and the underlying trend is not likely to persist. In these circumstances, there is a high likelihood of finding reversals, thus it would be worth considering.

Interest Rate Effects on Currencies

A. The Fundamental Accumulation and Distribution of Smart Money.

1) Interest rates are the single most significant factor driving market movements.

2) Making trade judgments may be aided by understanding interest rate shifts and changes.

3) Technical study of the main interest rates might reveal professional money flow.

4) Interest Triads provide a picture of how smart money gathers and is distributed.

Interest Rate Triads, part A

1) Key Long Term Interest Rate for 30 Year Bonds.

2) Intermediate Term Interest Rate on a 10 Year Note.

3) Short-Term Interest Rate on a 5 Year Note.

4) Unlocking Price Action requires overlaying or comparative analysis of these three Interest Rates. 5) Mistake Swings at opportune moments may confirm Institutional Order Flow

Interest Rate Triad

The 10 year note, 5 year note, and 30 year T bond markets are located here.

From a "Smart Money" perspective, overlaying these three markets will reveal when the interest rate market experiences accumulation and distribution. The three Interest Rates should support one another by making higher highs or lower lows when the USDX is at key price points. Failure swings prove that there is Smart Money in the markets and validate trading opportunities. Simply said, look for SMT Divergence.

Note: 10 Y T-Note UP == 10 Y T-bond UP == USDX DOWN == Interest Rates DOWN

Action Plan: As price approaches a focal area like orderblocks, liquidity voids, liquidity pool, or fair value gap, check USDX and Interest Rate Triads (30 Y T Bond Market, 10 Y T Note Market, 5 Y T Note Market) to see whether Smart Money is backing the trade idea you are seeing develop. If there are no signs that they are moving a lot of money, ignore them.

Liquidity Based Bias

Monthly, Weekly and Daily Charts all Bearish.

Day-by-Day Graphs It will correct or retrace higher in less than 4 hours. When this occurs, as you anticipate the market moving into a premium, you search for buy side liquidity to sell to. Possible effects include the filling of a Liquidity Void, fair value gaps, price reversals to bearish orderblocks, and protective buy stop raids. They are all offering possible Low Resistance Liquidity Runs, all of which are shorting for a target that is below a recent Low. Opposite of bullish

ICT LONG TERM ANALYSIS

The Quarterly Market Shifts: We expect a significant market movement every year that lasts for three to four months. In order to identify smart money distribution for sale programs and/or smart money accumulation for purchase programs, we assess the manipulation taking place in the underlying Vs. the benchmark. All that we look for is SMT divergence.

Additionally, a 20, 40, and 60 day look back is essential to identify institutional order movement utilizing recent institutional reference points, such as past price highs and lows, bearish orderblocks, bullish orderblocks, as well as gaps or voids in fair value.

Open Float

The current open interest above and below market price is referred to as "open float."

Stops for short protective buys should be set above recent bearish shifts, short-term highs, the highest high from the previous three months, the high from the current six-month period, and the high from the current yearlong period. It is the opposite for extended protective sell pauses.

Price and Treasury yield are inversely connected. When treasury prices decline, treasury yields increase and vice versa. Long-term investments look for returns. USDX may increase when yield declines and treasury prices increase, and the contrary is also true.

When the 10 Y T-Note and USDX move together, currencies will stabilize and show no patterns. Our primary goals in these circumstances are to halt raids and use the IPDA to go back in time and identify historical highs and lows that have been breached for USDX and T-Notes. During a consolidation, it is best to focus mostly on day trades as opposed to long-term trend trading.

If USDX and T Notes are moving in accordance with their regular seasonal patterns, which is where significant funds put their money, then we are most likely to be seeing a long-term trend.

Use SMT divergence in relation to the USDX to establish the ideal trading conditions for the 10 Y yields.

Interest Rate Differentials:

In the macro perspective, the interest rates of the central bank must come first. These interest rates are meant to stimulate or jump-start inflation in a country's economy. Finding a nation with a high IR and pairing it with one with a low IR is the long-term macro approach. The various currencies are fundamentally positioned for relative strength versus all other currencies when they are joined as a currency pair.

The converse is true for poorly matched countries with high IR coupled with a high IR country. These partnerships are fundamentally set up for weakness when compared to all other combinations.

Action Strategy: Decide on two countries, one with a high IR and the other with a low IR, and define the forex pair coupling for transactions. Seek for an HTF chart with strong backing. Look for indications that smart money is buying it. Use seasonal trends or professed desire to confirm. confirmation of the USDX's qualifying direction.

Vice versa for selling

Intermarket Analysis

Because word markets are interconnected, understanding them all at once makes analysis easier. The top four intermarket analysis groups are currencies, stock markets, bonds & interest rates, and commodities.

Stocks and bonds move in tandem. Contrary to bond prices, commodities fluctuate

Commodities have an impact on currencies.

USDX vs Commodities: They are inversely related.

USDX UP ➔ decrease in agricultural and grain exports, decline in stocks and bonds, and commodity
Currencies DOWN. :::::: *Vice versa is also true*

Bonds vs Commodities: They have a reverse relationship.

These have an emphasis on inflation.

Long-term changes have a lead period of 6–12 months.

T Bonds in comparison to the CRB Index (Heavy Ag and Grain Weighting)

Utilize the Energy Weighted Goldman Sachs Commodity Index.

Use the Goldman Sachs Industrial Index to monitor world developments.

Commodities UP Bond Yield UO, and vice versa.

Bond vs Stock Market: They are related in a good way.

Bond prices serve as a head start indication for stock movement.

Long-term lag or lead time in changes is 6–12 months.

Bonds do well during deflationary times as interest rates drop. Bonds higher than stocks and lower than commodities.

Key Intermarket Relationships:

USDX increased as gold decreased.

Gold Exports Up in Australia & New Zealand

OIL UP USDCAD DOWN (Leader in exports from Canada)

Nikkei UP > DOW UP

Downward trends in the Nikkei Index, the USDJPY, yields, and currency indicate that money is seeking yield.

USDCAD declines along with gold

These connections support long-term analysis as a whole.

Seasonal Tendencies

Seasonal patterns should be seen as a metaphorical "roadmap" of past accomplishment rather than as a panacea or the absolute truth. If the situation permits, they may be used, although they are seldom honored. Examine if the seasonal trend has any technical justifications.

TOP DOWN ANALYSIS

Markets go from bearish premium arrays to bullish discount arrays during bearish times, and vice versa.

The following is a list of the PD arrays in order of importance:

1. Mitigation Block.
2. . Liquidity Void.
3. Bullish/Bearish Breaker
4. Bullish/Bearish Order Block.
5. Fair Value Gap.
6. Rejection Block.
7. Old high/low.

Buying with Stop orders:

The following PD arrays are listed in order of importance: The pricing on a weekly and/or monthly basis should show that IOF will be searching for a PD array above the price on a daily basis.

The Daily should include a pessimistic candle with a bearish wick. The start of a bearish candle is where the buy stop is placed.

Conversely, if you sell using stop orders.

Limit order purchases should be made based on the weekly and/or monthly pricing, which should show that IOF will be searching for PD arrays above the daily market price.

On the daily chart, the candle must have a downward closing. At the conclusion of a bearish candle, the purchase limit is established.

Contrarily, selling using limit orders.

Bullish Market Conditions

i. Recognize any probable seasonal bullish inclination

ii. Seek verification from intermarket analysis

iii. To confirm, consult the IR Yields instruction.

4. Review the HTF Weekly & Monthly Chart for PDA.

v. Be prepared for an intermediate swing and a quarterly shift.

vii. Frame your bullish setup using the Daily PDA.

vii. Choose whether you'll enter by limit or stop.

viii. Place a trailing stop loss below the 40-day average low price.

Vice versa for bearish market conditions

SWING TRADING MODEL

systematically buying bullish and selling bearish market conditions in order to trade anticipated market price movements. Trades that last two weeks or more constitute the intermediate trading style known as swing trading.

Swing trading tries to make money from the effects of bigger firms entering a market and causing a significant price displacement. Gains might be large since transaction times could be as lengthy as two weeks. Trade objectives with a size of 200 to 500 pip may be beneficial for these situations.

Keep in mind that not all markets are good for swing trading setups and steer clear of your favorites in general. Significant changes occur in and out of several markets every year. A conventional swing trading pair or market doesn't exist. Every three months, there are fresh swing trading opportunities. What was a significant power before won't always be a major force now.

Market profiles are essential because markets fluctuate from one profile to the next throughout all time periods. On the weekly and monthly charts, look for the current market profile for your target markets. Avoid investing in markets that haven't changed significantly, if at all, during the preceding three months.

Due to their strong flows, trending markets should be sought for. Markets that clearly constrain their trading range do not provide a high likelihood for directional setups. Make a watch list of markets that offer setups with a high possibility that have monthly, weekly, or other trending market profiles.

By being prepared to err on the side of caution, one may avoid the temptation to forecast price peaks and bottoms. Price movement is significantly more likely to be influenced by the long-term moving market profile than by a long-term reversal. When you focus on the long-term trend, the market tide will typically carry your transaction into the black.

Successful swing trading hallmarks:

• Seasonal tendency (enhances likelihood)

• COT Data Confirms (enhances probability)

• Opposing PDA apparent in charts

• Apparent trend in HTF Charts

• IOF on HTF Clear

• IR Market supports the trade

Intermarket analysis support

Corporate Sponsorship: Do relative strength analysis indicators exist to aid in transactions when buying or selling?::: SMT divergence.

Bank accumulation and distribution: Are the down candles serving as support and seeing higher prices, or are the swing highs breaking and reaching higher highs? Are the ascending candles functioning as barriers when prices decline? Observe the swing lows breaking and the lower lows.

When the PDA is above or below the market price, it is clear and easy to detect. When a price is not transacted, does it leave a monthly and weekly basis out of balance? The markets with the clearest price action are the ones to trade on. Less chance that wrong price action would mislead or distract you. Price in line with the requirements of the institution: 00, 20 50 80.

Rule-based conceptual methods: each trade is subjected to a set of rules-based screening steps. The rules don't change with each different transaction setting; they are standard and constant. Trade setups are forwarded on if they don't pass the screening process. Never any exceptions. If the trade setups pass the screening process, the transaction is executed.

When the daily, weekly, and monthly sequences all point to a willingness to buy (buy Daily or H4 Bullish Array) or sell (sell Weekly or H4 Bearish Array), use the PD Array matrix. Don't purchase or sell if the daily previously recorded a higher high/lower low but was disregarded as a breaker. The greatest fluctuations occur at the weekly and monthly levels.

Selecting Explosive Moves:

i. One-sided major market analysis with trending profiles.

ii. Confluences in Intermarket Analysis

Alignment of the COT Hedging scheme.

iv. Seasonal tendency v. Open Interest

v. Contraction is confirmed by the volatility filter

vii.Important new headlines: Use futures magazines to sell bullish news and vice versa. William%R on a daily basis - 50% & lower is oversold buy, according to Markey emotion.

 Opposite for a sale.

SHORT TERM TRADING

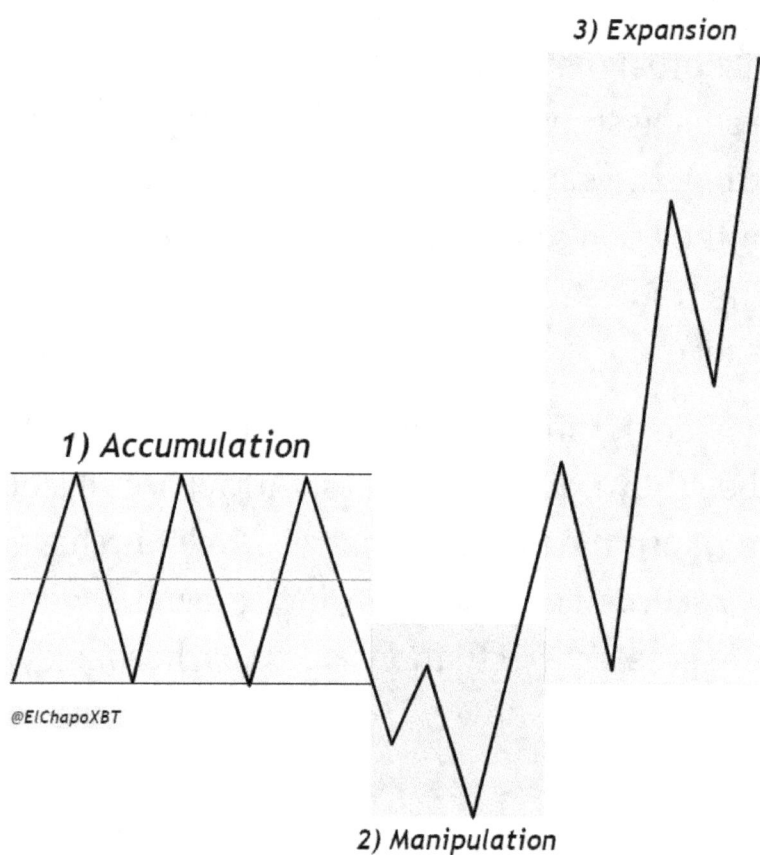

Hedging a week's worth of time across a few days. utilizing both weekly and monthly charts to build the setups. We make trades in the direction of the current or following week's range. Understanding the weekly range is essential.

Both the trend-based and range-based short-term models are viable. Making spontaneous deals, not forced ones, is the goal. Trading short-term is the discipline with the greatest possibility. Due to regularity and frequent setups, there are several trades possible.

When determining the market conditions during an upswing and a downswing, we take the price's probable range into account. The direction of the market is predicted using this as a starting point.

According to the most recent transactions or performances, the opposite PD Array spectrum will be reached. If the discount array has sustained the price, there is a greater chance that the premium array will as well, and vice versa. We look for a monthly PD array as opposed to a weekly PD array.

The execution time is H1.

The general Concept revisited:

On HTF, the market is expected to trade higher due to the following factors:

Seasonality;

Interest rate sensitivity;

Traders' commitment;

Intermarket analysis, which promotes bullishness.

Mon-Wed sees market rises followed by retracements.

The market rises to new highs.

Inverse to become bearish

Monthly ranges:

HTF Analysis is helpful since price is fractal. We note the High and Low on each Monthly candle. Note the premium or discount range at the moment. Consider potential future price increases. Typically, a monthly candle has 4 weekly candles. Every week, we do research on the next monthly trading location. We use the monthly ranges to arrange trades on the weekly range.

Weekly ranges:

The weekly analysis is developed on a monthly basis, and price is fractal. We note the peak and low on each weekly candle. Note the premium or discount range at the moment. Consider the potential appeal of the weekly price. Typically, there are 5 candles in each weekly candle. Every week, we do research on the weekly transactions in the monthly range. Deals are framed using weekly ranges on the daily chart.

It should be observed that when the Mon-Wed high/low is traded via Array, price often expands quickly toward the weekly or monthly PD.

Defining Weekly Range profiles and Templates:

Bullish: Traditional Tuesday low of the Week

Manipulation: To produce the week's low, the hover climbs above an HTF Discount Array on Monday before falling into the HTF Discount Array on Tuesday.

Know the HTF Discount Array; if the market doesn't fall into it on Tuesday, there's a good chance a drive down will occur. London or New York session.

Wednesday low of the Week: Bullish

Manipulation: Monday and Tuesday hovers above an HTF Discount Array, then Wednesday sinks into the HTF Discount Array to create the week's low.

Anticipation: Recognize the HTF Discount Array; if the market fails to join that array on Wednesday in either London or New York, a downward movement is likely to occur. These days, Monday and Tuesday, may likewise be sluggish ones.

Consolidation Thursday Reversal: Bullish

Manipulation: Monday through Wednesday's consolidation is followed by a run at the intraweek low and a rejection of it, which creates a market reversal.

Know the HTF Discount Array and anticipate that if the market doesn't dip into it on Thursday, it will likely decline due to news or a rate announcement in the late New York Session at about 2:00 EST.

Consolidation Midweek Rally: Bullish

Manipulation: consolidates from Monday through Wednesday, reaches its intraweek high, and then increases into Friday.

Anticipation: the market hasn't yet surged to the Premium Array on the HTF timeframes after recovering from a discount array and has just stagnated without any negative reversal Price Action. Signaling that a price rise for the premium array was imminent.

Seek and Destroy Bullish Friday: Bullish

The market consolidates from Monday through Thursday before starting to expand again on Friday. Shallow stops are used below and above the intraweek highs.

Expectation: This profile may be generated in the summer months of July and August, when the market is looking forward to an announcement about interest rates or an NFP report. When possible, steer clear of trading in these circumstances.

Wednesday Weekly Reversal: bullish

Manipulation: Consolidates from Monday through Tuesday, then sharply reverses downward into an HTF Discount Array to trigger Sell Stops.

Anticipation: With available sell-side liquidity, institutional buying will start when the market reaches a long- or intermediate-term low. Stop Raids, buy

Each week, the market will try to trade from one PD Array to the next. Typically, 30 to 50% of the weekly range falls between Monday and Wednesday.

Intra-Week Market Reversals and overlapping models:

Wednesday or Thursday might see the first of monthly reversals.

Given the magnitude of the price change on Monday and Tuesday, exercise caution; keep an eye on HTF Array as it may suddenly reverse.

Intraweek reversals are seen in overlapping models. Consequently, the HTF PD Array Matrix is important. It can offer swing or position trades to you.

HTF profile always prevails when market profiles clash.

One Shot One Kill Setups:

OSOK requires:

Using Weekly Candles or Ranges to Apply the Power of 3 Concept

Day of the Week Concept: High or Low Forms It happens between Monday and Wednesday 70% of the time.

Understanding the concept of price points and targeting using Fib.

Kill zones for entry are based on the time of day or ICT OSOK installations.

Everything that has been learned from the beginning.

OSOK Trade Procedure:

The present or probable next quarterly shift should be determined.

Find the IPDA Data Ranges' HTF PD Arrays.

Refer to Market Profile of Rates and Interest Rate Differentials.

Throughout the year, look for seasonals that provide odds.

Swing analysis of HTF's price movement for the last 60 minutes.

Expect specific Weekly profiles to develop.

Get ready for the manipulation by market makers based on your profile.

Establish price action PD ranges.

Watch for volatility to indicate a strong likelihood of wide ranges.

For confirmation of Smart Money activity, consult COT and Open Interest.

With opposing PD Arrays, frame a liquidity run with low resistance.

Utilize Fibs to converge with opposing IPDA Data Ranges for Time, Price, and PD Arrays. Utilize intermarket analysis to validate trade setups..

ICT DAY TRADING MODEL

Opportunities inside the Daily Range:

- The goal is to take advantage of the mobility that is present for just one day.
- Not every day is suitable for day trading.
- On average, there are two setups every trading day.

- The daily range should be quite similar to the five-day ADR.

- The majority of day trade setups use directional bias frames.

- Day trading with an eye on the weekly term is the best course of action.

- You can find more HTF strategies to help you day trade the batter.

- The trader can set a stop loss on all of their day transactions.

- It's crucial to avoid engaging in a lot of day transactions throughout a single 24-hour period.

- PD Arrays and IPDA Data Ranges form the framework.

- There are no live settings on FOMC and NFP days, keeping us off the field.

What frames Daily setups:

The HTF IOF.

- The IPDA is aiming for higher prices for liquidity.

- Current Candle direction on Weekly Chart.

Day of the week.

Hour of the day.

- Expansion of volatility, or "large daily ranges"

Date and Time:

• The London Session is open from 2:00 to 4:00 AM NY Time.

• New York Session Open: More user-friendly. Avoid London if the ADR is above 80%.

• Close to London

• New York Finish

• Open Asian Session

• Consolidation/continuation of the London Lunch into New York at 5:00–7:00 New York Time

Weekend Day:

Sunday: daily opt-out range is too narrow

Monday - might result in a limited range. typically

Tuesday is often an excellent trading day. Wednesday is often the best day for trading. Normally a good day, Thursday, may go wrong.

Friday is usually a tiny range that ends the week.

Weekly Range Framework:

In order to aid in day trading directional bias throughout the week, we establish the opening price for the forthcoming trading week on Sunday. A 60-minute chart is used to indicate the Sunday open.

When utilizing the Sunday beginning price filter and a negative weekly directional bias, we watch for price to cross over this level early in the week. As long as the price is below this Sunday starting price, we want to sell short in our day trades. prior to switching to an HTF PD array. The same is true for an optimistic weekly directional bias.

London should come first, then all of New York.

The opening price of large weekly range candles is at the range's opposing ends.

The Daily Range is Defined:

The MT4 interface shows the standard GMT daily divisions for the 24-hour trading day for retail customers. The 24-hour IPDA interbank day differs significantly. We must approach the market in a manner comparable to the IPDA.

The Asian Range Explained: The Asian Range starts every day at 8:00 p.m. EST in [NY].

Every day at Midnight, the Asian range finishes in [NY].

The ICT London KillZone: The London KillZone starts each day at 1:00 a.m. EST.

The London KillZone comes to an end each day at 5:00 EST.

The ICT New York KillZone (NY KZ) starts each day at 7:00 a.m. EST.

The NY KZ comes to a conclusion each day at 10:00 EST.

The London Close KillZone (LC KZ) starts each day at 10:00 EST.

The LC KZ comes to a conclusion each day at noon EST.

The IPDA True Day officially starts each day at 12:00 a.m. Eastern Time (EST).

The IPDA True Day comes to a close each day at 3:00 PM EST.

True Day is at midnight. NY

At 0 GMT, IPDA True Day is.

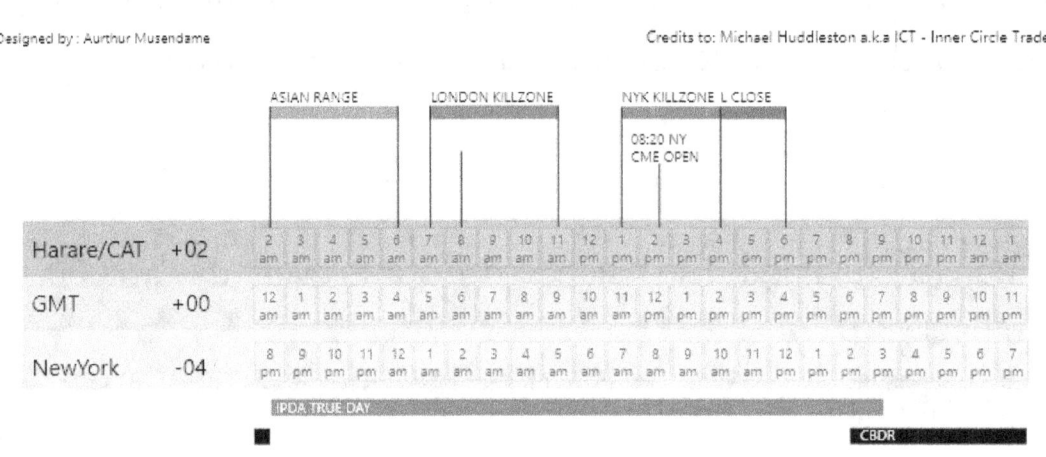

Designed by : Aurthur Musendame   Credits to: Michael Huddleston a.k.a ICT - Inner Circle Trader

Central Bank Dealers Range (CBDR): Daily Highs and Lows Projected

Time: 2:00 p.m. to 8:00 p.m. EST

The optimal range is between 20 and 30 pip, which is below 40 pip.

Forecasting is often inefficient for ranges bigger than 30 pip.

Both the distance in pips between the highest and lowest body and the distance between the high and low may be altered.

The CBDR facilitates the selection of a LOD or HOD.

CBDR creates two SDs on optimum sell days, and vice versa.

4 SDs higher if the HOD is reporting on a news event, and vice versa.

The use of projections should be combined with directional bias.

To project the expansion, you may utilize the full HOD. Judas swung projected SD plus CBDR as one SD.

Intra Day Market profiles

Sell Profile: London Normal protraction

The CBDR is not 40 pip or more.

The range in Asia is 20–30 pip.

After 12:00 am NY till 2:00 am NY, the market increases.

Judas Swing or the protraction state will be between one and two SDs of CBDR.

London Sell Profile Delayed Expansion

The CBDR of the market may or may not be favorable.

Although the protraction is delayed, the directional bias is bearish.

A protraction stage will begin for IPDA at or just after 2:00 am NY.

Watch for retracements in intraday premium PD Arrays to short on.

Likewise for BUY profiles.

When to Avoid the London Session

If the London session is not ideal, when?

• After a day with a wide range that exceeds two times the five-day ADR.

• Avoid far shots after three up-close shots in a row. Also the opposite.

• Following a FOMC event that causes severe whipsaws.

• Prior to Non-Farm Payroll figures.

• Trading is wrapping up for the day as a long weekend holiday approaches.

• Several news sources with high to medium effect in that market. (1 or 2) are suitable. • A "wildcard day" in London may occur when there are no newscasts.

What characteristics to do I look for?

• The CBDR has more than 50 pip. [Maybe omit London]

The Asian range is 40 pip points or more. Think about delayed protraction.

• The market starts to steadily increase or fall at 8:00 PM NY. [poor]

• When the CBDR or Asian range does not visibly converge. [Limited to London]

• Our goal is to reach the day when the bank will "hold" the market in order to create open float.

• The market becomes unstable if it trends from 8:00 p.m. in New York to 8:00 p.m. in London.

• Trade NYO in the morning when the market is primed for London garbage.

The day-to-day operations entail distribution, manipulation, and accumulation.

When is the London open KillZone Ideal?

• The daily graphic clearly shows respect for PD Arrays.

• The market recently responded to an HTF PD array without coming across an opposing PD array.

When the market for premium Arrays is anticipated to go higher everyday, London longs are the ideal choice. The same goes for trading losses. • A day of expansion is anticipated when the daily range has not recently surpassed its five-day ADR.

High Probability Day Trades Setups:

The HTF daily and/or H4 directive is given the utmost priority.

When the direction of the Daily and H4 is bullish, you should: • Enter retracements using the previous day's low to high.

• For retracement entry, use the NY session low to high from the previous day.

• To build up long positions, use the previous day's low for sell stop raids.

• Paying attention to the upcoming switch from HTF Discount to Premium PD Array.

Vice versa for Bearish

When do I look to buy day trades?

• Preferably during price-rising seasons, however this is not required.

• When there is a favorable prognosis for the current or next quarters.

• In the wake of a positive reaction on a discount PD Array from the daily chart.

• When there is a clear, unhindered route from pricing to a premium array that is competing.

• The best days of the week to purchase are Tuesday, Wednesday, and Monday.

• Determine if the CBDR is, ideally, less than 40 pip.

• Demand that the Asian range be in a 20 pip range before Frankfurt opens.

• Shopping for LOD between 2:00 and 4:00 AM New York Time.

• Get a cheap PDA and a couple CBDR and/or Asian Range SD cards.

• The chart execution period of 15 or 5 minutes.

Where do I look to buy day trades?

• Plus five pip above the Asian range.
• FVG dropped below the day's prior short-term low for the NY Session.
• A block of bullish orders under a recent or active short-term low.
• If I'm extremely bullish, 1 SD with ANY Discount PD Array in LO KillZone.
• Using a PDA, from midnight to two in the morning, decrease post
• The filling of a liquidity hole that takes place below a transient low.
• Purchase the first retracement into a 15- or 5-minute OB if a gain happens after midnight.
• Asian-range discount PD array coupled with 1-2 SD.
• Purchase turtle soup if the short-term low is twice reached without improvement.

Placing Stop-Losses in Buy Day Trades?

• Take your time moving whatever first stop loss you decide to utilize.

• Your stop should be 30 pip below if you are trading the CBDR when it overlaps with the PD Array.

• The stop is 40 pip under if you are trading a run under the Asian range.

• If you are trading any securities, place your sell stop raid 30 pip below the low or entry.

• 10 pip beneath LOD if you are trading the initial retracement into OB.

• 30 pip under LOD for sell stops when trading second returns

• If you are trading any other setup not covered above, subtract the Asian range low by 50% ADR from the past five days.

Taking profits in Buy Day Trades.

   • Always aim to remove anything in 20 to 30 pip increments. Always.

   • A scale that subtracts two SDs from the Asian range or CBDR.

   • Deduct something at the day's high plus 5 to 15 pip.

   • Reduce a price by 50% inside the 60-second trading window. • Take or receive discounts of 60–80% at 5-day ADR forecasts. Always.

   • Take something off if the price is trading higher than the prior trading month or week high.

   • Scale out at 5:00 am New York time. Period of time

   • Scale out at the short-term high before 7:00 a.m. NYO.

   • Scale out in rallies from 10:00 to 11:00 am New York time.

- The ideal combination is any of the aforementioned events with a Premium PD Array.

Vice versa for Short Day Trades

Integrating Day Trades with HTF Trade Entries:

- We may position our longer-term HTF trades using day trading entries.

- A technique exists that takes very little time and analysis.

- If you can't trade it, we don't need to utilize the London KillZone.

- IPDA uses "reset" to describe two key periods of the day.

- For all types of trading, the daily candle might provide the best entry positions.

PO3: open → rally/decline → close

The Openings or The Open.

Every day, you should pay attention to two session "openings":

- 0 GMT - Common basis for calibration across the world. • 12:01 a.m. New York time.

There are sophisticated access points that are available in the open.

They are not required to position using Day Trading Concepts on HTF setups.

Imagine being able to maintain a position for a lot longer and earning more pip rewards by trading the Daily Range for a single day.

Only the first cost must be understood. Buy at 0 GMT on days that are bullish, and vice versa. Put an end to the five-day ADR.

ICT AMPLIFIED DAY TRADING MODEL AND SCALPING

The sentiment Effect:

When are there the best opportunities to buy or sell?

For day traders, using the Asian range and beginning price is essential.

Bearish Short days: Ideally, above either the opening price or the high of the Asian range.

Ideally, the Asian range bottom or the opening price should be below the bullish long days.

Less experienced traders would chase the price on the impulse or early intraday movement as a result of short-term changes in the market's "Sentiment."

If you focus on strict limitations like Daily or 4h direction based in IOF and combine the PD Array matrix for next level targets, you will have the greatest probability configurations.

We hold off on entering trades in the market's opposite direction for setups with high likelihood.

Purchase Requirements: Proper Setups for Long Entries

• A Daily or minimum $H Discount Array is predicted by the IPDA.

• On the daily or at least four-hour chart, there is a substantial number of pip between the opposing Premium Array and market price.

• Both the "Opening Price" and the Asian Range Low are surpassed.

• In a perfect world, a fall down the Asian range low would lead to a reasonable discount range on the 15 minute period.

• Prices at the discount array often don't persist for more than 15 minutes.

• Be ready for the price to significantly increase after it is beyond the 15-minute discount range.

• The longer a price is at or near the 15-minute discount zone, the lower the odds. • Short-term sentiment will be at its most negative when we begin long trading.

Utilize a 10-period W%r for emotion.

In contrast, brief entries

Filling the Numbers

IPDA searches for fill 4 numbers every day.

Each day, the daily range will try to fill or trade at four distinct levels.

day's low or high before

In excess of the central pivot: R1, R4, R2, M5, R3, and M3

Following the pivot's center: M3, S1, M1, S2, M0, S3.

Using the PD Array Matrix and order flow direction to create a particular bias.

When choosing entry points for trades, search for fillable numbers.

• If you have a lengthy entry, check above it for the consecutive 4 levels above. • For short entries, check the successive 4 levels below your input.

More than four levels may be filled on days with a big range.

A general guideline is to advance through at least four levels.

Once four levels have filled, you should preferably close out the bulk of your trade position.

If you have the time, leave some on in case the day might have a broad range of weather.

Order flow direction and the PD Array Matrix for a certain bias

• Taking advantage of the CBDR while shorting the market: If you sell over the CBDR, you regard the low as the first of four levels that need to be filled. The market will probably fall to four CBDR lows. • When buying below the Asian range utilizing the Asian range, you consider the Asian range's highest level as level one or level four to fill. In the Asian region, the market might reach up to four highs. Reverse for Shorting

• The flout range to the high equilibrium is counted as one SD when utilizing the flout to short the market or short above the flout equilibrium. The equilibrium of the full range and the low are separated by one SD. Using 50% of the whole flout range, or between 3 p.m. and 12 a.m. in New York, the entire flout range is forecast. It is projected that the market would fall to four range lows. VARSE VASAR FOR BUY

Which figures do you emphasize?

When deciding which numbers to fill, keep in mind that we can never be certain of the levels IPDA will use before the trading day starts.

We could get a little bit closer to reality as the trading day draws to a conclusion.

The New York Session will typically offer the measurements that IPDA is currently using for the engineering of the daily range.

We look for points where one or more of the techniques we use to evaluate the four levels meet. By combining these factors with the current trading environment, time of day, direction, and PDA Matrix, you may predict the anticipated Daily High or Low.

striving for 20 pip each day

You will never be able to earn 20 pip each day.

Your goal for each day deal you do should be to gain 20 pip.

However, there are a few techniques that may be used to almost always detect a 20 pip scalp. (Impl. "almost").

To comprehend the situation of the market, the trader needs still perform study. expanding, turning around, and combining.

Yen, Au, Kiwi, and Crosses are exchanged for 15-minute NY Session Stops.

Buy Setup: Keep an eye out for recent lows that were hit in the NY Session up to 12:00 am New York time during the Asian session. for shorts, turn around

Trading all pairs for the New York Expansion Setup is allowed up to ten o'clock in New York. Trading continues long after NY tries the lows since 5 ADR pending were posted in London and NY time hunts short-term lows created at the NY Open Daily Low. For shorts, turn around.

Utilizing a 5-minute time chart. The target has been established at 20 pip the 20 pip stop.

The Secret behind consolidations:

Retail traders: They'll watch for a breakthrough to build a bias in one way.

Smart Money: Will design or downplay consolidation breakouts.

Retail traders: They purchase at the previous low and sell at the prior high.

The wise investor buys at previous lows and sells at previous highs.

Chase expansions that come from the equilibrium, retail traders.

Smart money says to diminish the expansions that result from equilibrium.

Trading Market Reversals:

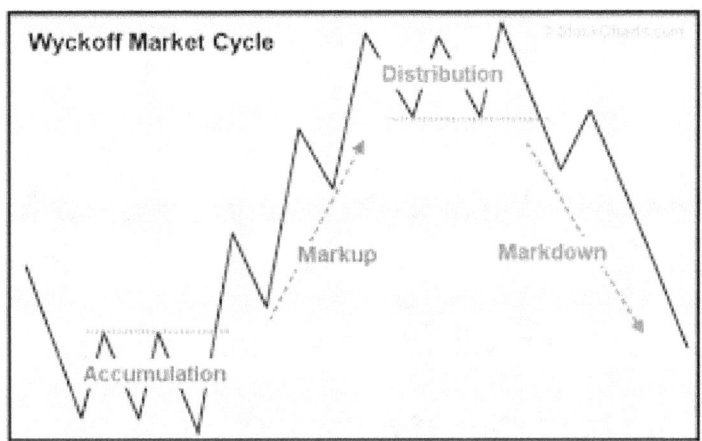

Eight reversals that may be traded successfully include:

• Raid buy stops at the previous day's high and reverse.

• Raid Sell Stops at Yesterday's Low and Reverse.

• Intra-Week High: Reverse and Raid Buy Stops.

• Raid Sell Stops and Reverse at Intra-Week Low.

• Intermediate Term High: Reverse and Raid Buy Stops.

• Intermediate Term Low: Reverse and Raid Sell Stops.

• Reversals of New York Sessions [Utilize regular templates]

• Reversals of the London Close. [on Days with Large Range > 5ADR]

Bread and Butter Buy Setups:

Daily Opportunities for Scalping: In purchase programs, IPDA will run one of two price engine models:

1. Increase sell-side liquidity by repricing under a previous low.

• Counterparty sellers are asked to match lengthy entry with sell stops when they are enabled.

• Price will search for a larger short-term Premium Array to balance holdings.

2. Re-accumulate fair value at a discount in arrays with smaller retracements.

• The lower retracement will limit weak long holders.

• The price will strive to increase to a short-term premium range in order to balance holdings.

Offset Accumulation: IPDA will reprice the market below an Old Low in order to encourage Sell Stops that would be situated there for current Long holders. Essentially, this "engineers" Sellers to provide goods at significant discounts. The open float below that Old Low can include sell stops for breakout systems that also sell on weakness.

This model is called offset accumulation. Its major objective is to "Offset" current long holders and/or persuade additional sellers to provide special pricing. The model is often witnessed when the market is bullish and the HTF IOF is signaling higher prices.

Since offset accumulation models often form quickly, you must be able to foresee them at critical intraday lows.

Reaccumulation: IPDA will reprice the market to a Fair Value price range in order to deliver Smart Money discount pricing for prolonged entry. It seems sense that after a recent Sell Stop Raid, the market would go in a positive direction. The price drop will affect those who are currently holding long positions and is likely to cause selling, providing sell side liquidity to coincide with long entries from smart money.

This idea is referred to as reaccumulation. Its major objective is to "reaccumulate" long entries already submitted and/or to entice new vendors by providing them with special pricing. The model is often witnessed when the market is bullish and the HTF IOF is signaling higher prices.

Reaccumulation models often form quickly, therefore you must learn to spot them at significant intraday lows.

Set attainable objectives.

The average duration of a trade is 1-2 hours or less.

15 to 30 pip on average every deal.

Timing of the Chary interval: 5 minutes.

A maximum of 15 or more setups are made each week.

2 to 3 setups each day typically

One of each session (Asia, LO, NYO, and LC)

Typically, the risk to return ratio is at least 1:1.

The recommended risk per transaction is from 0.5% to 1%.

The only time that scalping is permitted is during ICT KillZones.

Because the length and style of trading are so short term in nature, we need to "get a move" at the most volatile times of the day.

An entry may sometimes execute outside of a KillZone when using limit orders. This typically happens after NYO or during London Lunch. It's crucial to be up to date with the market if you want to scalp intraday.

Revisiting the Daily Range:

In conclusion, when the market is prepared to trade higher based on HTF IOF, we expect the Open to be around or near the daily range low.

It's conceivable for prices to drop somewhat to the open price or lower.

London Open records the first leg higher intraday before waiting for NYO.

Prices for NYO are anticipated to increase until 10:00 New York time.

At 10:00 am and Noon, NY Time, respectively, the Daily Range High and the 5 Day ADR Projected High are anticipated to take place.

Frequently, the price will turn around and close off the day's high.

The London Open:

1. When HTF IOF is bullish, we seek for the London session bottom of the day formation.

2. At the open at 0 GMT, or 12 am in New York, a lower price for a protraction phase may be seen. This might be scalped from the Open or just above it before 1:00 am NY time.

3. It's easier to scalp the typical London Judas Swing lower.

4. The market retraces between 5:00 and 7:00 am NY time after a Discount Array is reached, which may provide an opportunity for a long scalp entry.

5. To win the remaining London open till 5:00 am NY time, take a 5-minute retracement after the ideal Judas entry timing has gone.

The New York Session:

1. Unless an HTF premium Array has been struck intraday or an ADR is achieved, we anticipate to see NYO go higher after London Open verifies institutional sponsorship on the long side and posts the daily low.

2. To select Discount range arrays to go long in the NYO KillZone, we check for intraday moves upward.

3. Predicting the NY Judas swing to fade using the CME Open time of 8:20 am NY.

4. On the 4H, 60 min basis, the next HTF Premium Array and the ADR High will be the targets.

5. If ADR is achieved before 10:00 am, cut down on the amount by 80% while leaving a tiny amount on to account for any potential range extension.

The London Close:

1. After the NY and London Sessions have climbed in sync, the 5 day ADR has been reached, and it is at least 10:30 am NY time, anticipate a retreat from the day's high. 10:30 - 1:00 pm

2. Ideally, the price should be higher than 1.25 percent of the% day ADR range.

3. Keep an eye out for a bearish OB to enter on and a failure of a 5-minute swing at the high.

4. Taking a 10-pip risk above the day's high and aiming for a retracement lower of 20–30% of the total daily range.

5. Keep in mind that the range may extend considerably farther than ADR High, making it impossible to predict how this strategy would perform on certain days.

6. Determine a 1:1 goal based on the required stop that is no larger than 20 pip.

The Asian open:

1. When the Asian range is constructed, we should expect a 15-20 pip rise if we join at or just below the 0 GMT Open price in a bullish market.

2. Asian Sessions have a reputation for being rather tight, and although while this trade has historically been profitable, similar

to trades on the London Close, we are looking at the Daily Range formation at its least volatile points.

3. Always strive for gains of 15 to 20 pip in this session since the range may be limited owing to Asian range improvement.

4. Complete scalp escapes should be made at this time of day.

5. It's not ideal to anticipate a second leg in price. If you're fortunate enough to get 20 pip, don't become greedy and simply be pleased and go on.

Reverse for offset distribution and redistribution.

The Average Daily Range:

• The ADR is NOT need to be filled for the day.

• In certain circumstances, ADR may be anticipated to function as half of the real ADR:

o A significant impulsive swing may increase the daily range by double the ADR when a protracted trend is in motion and an intermediate-term swing has started, particularly when the ADR is less than 60 pip.

o Capitulation occurs when an intermediate-term swing reaches an HTF Array and is supported by High Impact News Events.

• ADR are good during London Close but not at NY Open.

• If High Impact News is expected out after stocks open, ADR will likely be surpassed if ADR fills at or before NYO.

The Scalping Model:

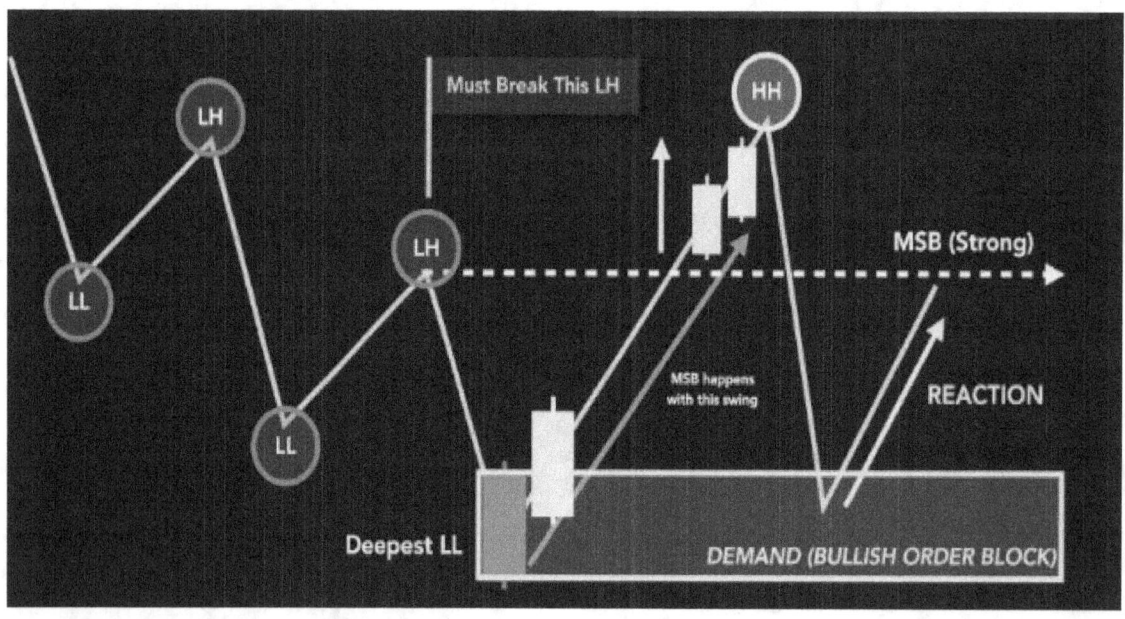

The setups are basically micro-setups on the 5 minute charts that we detail on the HTF charts.

The intraday price changes within each daily range must be framed by the time of day variables.

The HTF PD Arrays will pull price, however the intraday LTF PD Arrays do not provide the time or levels to enter on.

When the market is calm or it is too late to enter a transaction at the lowest risk, scalping is best used.

If you take the time to determine if the HTF is moving up or down and wait for small range days to form, the market will reward your patience by giving you daily ranges that expand and produce distinct intraday swings perfect for scalping.

www.ingramcontent.com/pod-product-compliance
Lightning Source LLC
Chambersburg PA
CBHW082227290526
45794CB00009B/3701